International Survey of Academic Library Data Curation Practices

ISBN: 978-1-57440-245-2
Library of Congress Control Number: 2013944899
© 2013 Primary Research Group, Inc.

TABLE OF CONTENTS

TABLE OF CONTENTS 3
LIST OF TABLES 4
THE QUESTIONNAIRE 10
THE QUESTIONNAIRE 10
SURVEY PARTICIPANTS 13
CHARACTERISTISCS OF THE SAMPLE 14
SUMMARY OF MAIN FINDINGS 15
1. Relations with Faculty on Data Curation Issues 22
2. Resources for Data Curation 29
3. Personnel 36
4. Data Storage 42
5. Data Integrity 44
6. Assessment and Information Resources 59

LIST OF TABLES

Table 1.1: Does the library offer advice to faculty on how to develop data management plans for grant proposals or personal use?......22

Table 1.2: Does the library offer advice to faculty on how to develop data management plans for grant proposals or personal use? Broken out by country.......22

Table 1.3: Does the library offer advice to faculty on how to develop data management plans for grant proposals or personal use? Broken out by full-time equivalent enrollment.......22

Table 1.4: Does the library offer advice to faculty on how to develop data management plans for grant proposals or personal use? Broken out by Carnegie Class (or equivalent).......22

Table 1.5: Does the library offer any one-on-one tutorials to train faculty in data management?......23

Table 1.6: Does the library offer any one-on-one tutorials to train faculty in data management? Broken out by country.......23

Table 1.7: Does the library offer any one-on-one tutorials to train faculty in data management? Broken out by full-time equivalent enrollment.......23

Table 1.8: Does the library offer any one-on-one tutorials to train faculty in data management? Broken out by Carnegie Class (or equivalent).......23

Table 1.9: Does the library offer any formal classes to train faculty in data management?......24

Table 1.10: Does the library offer any formal classes to train faculty in data management? Broken out by country.......24

Table 1.11: Does the library offer any formal classes to train faculty in data management? Broken out by full-time equivalent enrollment.......24

Table 1.12: Does the library offer any formal classes to train faculty in data management? Broken out by Carnegie Class (or equivalent)......24

Table 1.13: Does the library offer any workshops or seminars to train faculty in data management?......25

Table 1.14: Does the library offer any workshops or seminars to train faculty in data management? Broken out by country.......25

Table 1.15: Does the library offer any workshops or seminars to train faculty in data management? Broken out by full-time equivalent enrollment.......25

Table 1.16: Does the library offer any workshops or seminars to train faculty in data management? Broken out by Carnegie Class (or equivalent).......25

Table 1.17: Does the library offer any videos or web-based tutorials to train faculty in data management?......26

Table 1.18: Does the library offer any videos or web-based tutorials to train faculty in data management? Broken out by country.......26

Table 1.19: Does the library offer any videos or web-based tutorials to train faculty in data management? Broken out by full-time equivalent enrollment.......26

Table 1.20:	Does the library offer any videos or web-based tutorials to train faculty in data management? Broken out by Carnegie Class (or equivalent).	26
Table 2.1:	What percentage of the college/university overall spending on data curation would you say is contributed by the library?	29
Table 2.2:	What percentage of the college/university overall spending on data curation would you say is contributed by the library? Broken out by country.	29
Table 2.3:	What percentage of the college/university overall spending on data curation would you say is contributed by the library? Broken out by full-time equivalent enrollment.	29
Table 2.4:	What percentage of the college/university overall spending on data curation would you say is contributed by the library? Broken out by Carnegie Class (or equivalent).	29
Table 2.5:	Has the library ever received an external grant to support activities in data curation?	30
Table 2.6:	Has the library ever received an external grant to support activities in data curation? Broken out by country.	30
Table 2.7:	Has the library ever received an external grant to support activities in data curation? Broken out by full-time equivalent enrollment.	30
Table 2.8:	Has the library ever received an external grant to support activities in data curation? Broken out by Carnegie Class (or equivalent).	30
Table 3.1:	Have you hired or assigned librarians specifically to work on data curation issues?	36
Table 3.2:	Have you hired or assigned librarians specifically to work on data curation issues? Broken out by country.	36
Table 3.3:	Have you hired or assigned librarians specifically to work on data curation issues? Broken out by full-time equivalent enrollment.	36
Table 3.4:	Have you hired or assigned librarians specifically to work on data curation issues? Broken out by Carnegie Class (or equivalent).	36
Table 3.5:	Does your library have a data curation staff assigned specifically to deal with this issue?	37
Table 3.6:	Does your library have a data curation staff assigned specifically to deal with this issue? Broken out by country.	37
Table 3.7:	Does your library have a data curation staff assigned specifically to deal with this issue? Broken out by full-time equivalent enrollment.	37
Table 3.8:	Does your library have a data curation staff assigned specifically to deal with this issue? Broken out by Carnegie Class (or equivalent).	37
Table 3.9:	If the library has a data curation staff, how many FTE positions have been assigned to this staff or department?	38
Table 3.10:	If the library has a data curation staff, how many FTE positions have been assigned to this staff or department? Broken out by country.	38

Table 3.11:	If the library has a data curation staff, how many FTE positions have been assigned to this staff or department? Broken out by full-time equivalent enrollment.	38
Table 3.12:	If the library has a data curation staff, how many FTE positions have been assigned to this staff or department? Broken out by Carnegie Class (or equivalent).	38
Table 3.13:	Is there a distinct line item in your library budget for data curation?	39
Table 3.14:	Is there a distinct line item in your library budget for data curation? Broken out by country.	39
Table 3.15:	Is there a distinct line item in your library budget for data curation? Broken out by full-time equivalent enrollment.	39
Table 3.16:	Is there a distinct line item in your library budget for data curation? Broken out by Carnegie Class (or equivalent).	39
Table 3.17:	Do you believe that recent MLS graduates hired by the library have been adequately versed in data curation issues?	40
Table 3.18:	Do you believe that recent MLS graduates hired by the library have been adequately versed in data curation issues? Broken out by country.	40
Table 3.19:	Do you believe that recent MLS graduates hired by the library have been adequately versed in data curation issues? Broken out by full-time equivalent enrollment.	40
Table 3.20:	Do you believe that recent MLS graduates hired by the library have been adequately versed in data curation issues? Broken out by Carnegie Class (or equivalent).	40
Table 3.21:	What is the total number of grant proposals that have been reviewed or contributed to by your data curation office or service in the past year?	41
Table 3.22:	What is the total number of grant proposals that have been reviewed or contributed to by your data curation office or service in the past year? Broken out by country.	41
Table 3.23:	What is the total number of grant proposals that have been reviewed or contributed to by your data curation office or service in the past year? Broken out by full-time equivalent enrollment.	41
Table 3.24:	What is the total number of grant proposals that have been reviewed or contributed to by your data curation office or service in the past year? Broken out by Carnegie Class (or equivalent).	41
Table 4.1:	How are your data sets largely stored?	42
Table 4.2:	How are your data sets largely stored? Broken out by country.	42
Table 4.3:	How are your data sets largely stored? Broken out by full-time equivalent enrollment.	42
Table 4.4:	How are your data sets largely stored? Broken out by Carnegie Class (or equivalent).	42
Table 4.5:	How do you approach integrated data set retrieval?	43
Table 4.6:	How do you approach integrated data set retrieval? Broken out by country.	43

Table 4.7:	How do you approach integrated data set retrieval? Broken out by full-time equivalent enrollment	43
Table 4.8:	How do you approach integrated data set retrieval? Broken out by Carnegie Class (or equivalent)	43
Table 5.1:	Does the library have a data preservation strategy through which it has decided to maintain data for a minimum number of years?	45
Table 5.2:	Does the library have a data preservation strategy through which it has decided to maintain data for a minimum number of years? Broken out by country.	45
Table 5.3:	Does the library have a data preservation strategy through which it has decided to maintain data for a minimum number of years? Broken out by full-time equivalent enrollment	45
Table 5.4:	Does the library have a data preservation strategy through which it has decided to maintain data for a minimum number of years? Broken out by Carnegie Class (or equivalent).	45
Table 5.5:	How easy has it been to procure and archive notes or logs from scientific/social science experiments?	46
Table 5.6:	How easy has it been to procure and archive notes or logs from scientific/social science experiments? Broken out by country.	46
Table 5.7:	How easy has it been to procure and archive notes or logs from scientific/social science experiments? Broken out by full-time equivalent enrollment.	46
Table 5.8:	How easy has it been to procure and archive notes or logs from scientific/social science experiments? Broken out by Carnegie Class (or equivalent).	46
Table 5.9:	How easy has it been to procure and archive output or results from medical or scientific instruments or other monitors?	47
Table 5.10:	How easy has it been to procure and archive output or results from medical or scientific instruments or other monitors? Broken out by country.	47
Table 5.11:	How easy has it been to procure and archive output or results from medical or scientific instruments or other monitors? Broken out by full-time equivalent enrollment.	47
Table 5.12:	How easy has it been to procure and archive output or results from medical or scientific instruments or other monitors? Broken out by Carnegie Class (or equivalent).	47
Table 5.13:	How easy has it been to procure and archive video, photographs, or other images?	48
Table 5.14:	How easy has it been to procure and archive video, photographs, or other images? Broken out by country.	48
Table 5.15:	How easy has it been to procure and archive video, photographs, or other images? Broken out by full-time equivalent enrollment.	48
Table 5.16:	How easy has it been to procure and archive video, photographs, or other images? Broken out by Carnegie Class (or equivalent).	48
Table 5.17:	How easy has it been to procure and archive spreadsheets?	49

Table 5.18:	How easy has it been to procure and archive spreadsheets? Broken out by country.	49
Table 5.19:	How easy has it been to procure and archive spreadsheets? Broken out by full-time equivalent enrollment.	49
Table 5.20:	How easy has it been to procure and archive spreadsheets? Broken out by Carnegie Class (or equivalent).	49
Table 5.21:	How easy has it been to procure and archive databases?	50
Table 5.22:	How easy has it been to procure and archive databases? Broken out by country.	50
Table 5.23:	How easy has it been to procure and archive databases? Broken out by full-time equivalent enrollment.	50
Table 5.24:	How easy has it been to procure and archive databases? Broken out by Carnegie Class (or equivalent).	50
Table 5.25:	How easy has it been to procure and archive software code?	51
Table 5.26:	How easy has it been to procure and archive software code? Broken out by country.	51
Table 5.27:	How easy has it been to procure and archive software code? Broken out by full-time equivalent enrollment.	51
Table 5.28:	How easy has it been to procure and archive software code? Broken out by Carnegie Class (or equivalent).	51
Table 5.29:	How easy has it been to develop metadata for notes or logs from scientific/social science experiments?	52
Table 5.30:	How easy has it been to develop metadata for notes or logs from scientific/social science experiments? Broken out by country.	52
Table 5.31:	How easy has it been to develop metadata for notes or logs from scientific/social science experiments? Broken out by full-time equivalent enrollment.	52
Table 5.32:	How easy has it been to develop metadata for notes or logs from scientific/social science experiments? Broken out by Carnegie Class (or equivalent).	52
Table 5.33:	How easy has it been to develop metadata for output or results from medical or scientific instruments or other monitors?	53
Table 5.34:	How easy has it been to develop metadata for output or results from medical or scientific instruments or other monitors? Broken out by country.	53
Table 5.35:	How easy has it been to develop metadata for output or results from medical or scientific instruments or other monitors? Broken out by full-time equivalent enrollment.	53
Table 5.36:	How easy has it been to develop metadata for output or results from medical or scientific instruments or other monitors? Broken out by Carnegie Class (or equivalent).	53
Table 5.37:	How easy has it been to develop metadata for video, photographs, or other images?	54
Table 5.38:	How easy has it been to develop metadata for video, photographs, or other images? Broken out by country.	54

Table 5.39:	How easy has it been to develop metadata for video, photographs, or other images? Broken out by full-time equivalent enrollment.	54
Table 5.40:	How easy has it been to develop metadata for video, photographs, or other images? Broken out by Carnegie Class (or equivalent).	54
Table 5.41:	How easy has it been to develop metadata for spreadsheets?	55
Table 5.42:	How easy has it been to develop metadata for spreadsheets? Broken out by country.	55
Table 5.43:	How easy has it been to develop metadata for spreadsheets? Broken out by full-time equivalent enrollment.	55
Table 5.44:	How easy has it been to develop metadata for spreadsheets? Broken out by Carnegie Class (or equivalent).	55
Table 5.45:	How easy has it been to develop metadata for databases?	56
Table 5.46:	How easy has it been to develop metadata for databases? Broken out by country.	56
Table 5.47:	How easy has it been to develop metadata for databases? Broken out by full-time equivalent enrollment.	56
Table 5.48:	How easy has it been to develop metadata for databases? Broken out by Carnegie Class (or equivalent).	56
Table 5.49:	How easy has it been to develop metadata for software code?	57
Table 5.50:	How easy has it been to develop metadata for software code? Broken out by country.	57
Table 5.51:	How easy has it been to develop metadata for software code? Broken out by full-time equivalent enrollment.	57
Table 5.52:	How easy has it been to develop metadata for software code? Broken out by Carnegie Class (or equivalent).	57

THE QUESTIONNAIRE

RELATIONS WITH FACULTY ON DATA CURATION ISSUES

1. Does the library offer advice to faculty on how to develop data management plans for grant proposals or personal use?

2. Does the library offer any _____ to train faculty in data management?

    A. One-on-one tutorials
    B. Formal classes
    C. Workshops or seminars
    D. Videos or web-based tutorials

3. Describe your institution's data curation information literacy efforts and support efforts.

RESOURCES FOR DATA CURATION

4. What percentage of the college/university overall spending on data curation would you say is contributed by the library?

5. Has the library ever received an external grant to support activities in data curation?

6. Describe your library's relations with other players in data curation, such as the college/university office of grants management, or the academic departments that use the data curation services. Do they understand the library's efforts? Are there turf battles? What is the overall level of cooperation?

7. Since many grants now require a data curation strategy, and many departments of a college may be involved in this effort, the cost of this effort should be shared among these departmental players. Is this the case at your institution? If so, how do the contributions and roles break down? Has the library been given extra funds to carry out its data curation role?

8. Which academic fields would you say take most advantage of the data curation services offered by the library?

PERSONNEL

9. Have you hired or assigned librarians specifically to work on data curation issues?

10. Does your library have a data curation staff assigned specifically to deal with this issue?

11. If the library has a data curation staff, how many FTE positions have been assigned to this staff or department?

12. Is there a distinct line item in your library budget for data curation?

13. Do you believe that recent MLS graduates hired by the library have been adequately versed in data curation issues?

14. What is the total number of grant proposals that have been reviewed or contributed to by your data curation office or service in the past year?

DATA STORAGE

15. How are your data sets largely stored?

    A. Cloud computing service
    B. Library's server
    C. Some other college/university server

16. How do you approach integrated data set retrieval?

    A. We use an open source solution
    B. We use a commercial product
    C. We have developed our own home-grown approach

DATA INTEGRITY

17. At your institution, have you had any data curation disasters in which critical data was lost, destroyed, impermissibly accessed, or otherwise rendered far less useful than it might have been with more adequate curation measures? Keeping in mind that responses are not connected to institutions or respondents, can you describe some of these instances?

18. Does the library have a data preservation strategy through which it has decided to maintain data for a minimum number of years?

19. How easy has it been to procure and archive _____?

    A. Notes or logs from scientific/social science experiments
    B. Output or results from medical or scientific instruments or other monitors
    C. Video, photographs, or other images
    D. Spreadsheets
    E. Databases
    F. Software code

20. How easy has it been to develop metadata for _____?

A. Notes or logs from scientific/social science experiments
B. Output or results from medical or scientific instruments or other monitors
C. Video, photographs, or other images
D. Spreadsheets
E. Databases
F. Software code

21. How have you gone about developing metadata for your data curation efforts?

ASSESSMENT AND INFORMATION RESOURCES

22. How have your library's data curation activities impacted the standing and scholarly results of your institution? Have you made efforts to assess the impact of the data curation activities on institutional success?

23. What are some of the data archives or directories that you have found most useful in your data curation pursuits?

24. Which blogs, listservs, websites, magazines, newsletters, conferences, and other information resources have you found most useful in your data curation activities?

25. Which institutions do you most admire for their data curation efforts?

SURVEY PARTICIPANTS

Case Western Reserve University
Colorado State University
Dublin City University
George Mason University
Gogebic Community College
Griffith University
Indiana University-Purdue University Indianapolis
Lincoln University
London School of Economics and Political Science
Monash University
Oregon State University
Purdue University
Rutgers University
Saint Louis University
Southampton Solent University
Stockholm University
Suan Sunandha Rajabhat University
Trinity University
Tulane University
University of Arizona
University of California, Santa Cruz
University of Connecticut
University of Minnesota
University of Nevada-Las Vegas
University of Otago
University of Strathclyde
University of Victoria
University of Virginia
Uppsala University
Virginia Commonwealth University

CHARACTERISTISCS OF THE SAMPLE

Overall sample size: 30

By Country
United States	18
Other[1]	12

By FTE Student Enrollment
Less than 15,000	10
15,000 to 29,999	9
30,000 or more	11

By Carnegie Class (or Equivalent)[2]
RU/VH or top 150 ranking	16
RU/H or top 400 ranking	7
Other	7

---

[1] Australia, Canada, England, Ireland, New Zealand, Scotland, Sweden, and Thailand

[2] All US-based institutions are classified using the Carnegie Classification system. Research universities with "very high research activity" are classified as RU/VH, while RU/H indicates those institutions with "high research activity." For non-US institutions, these classifications are approximated according to the institution's world rank, courtesy of the Academic Ranking of World Universities (ARWU). All US institutions in the survey that are not RU/VH or RU/H, as well as all non-US institutions not ranked in the top 400 globally, fall under the category of "other."

SUMMARY OF MAIN FINDINGS

RELATIONS WITH FACULTY ON DATA CURATION ISSUES

Developing Data Management Plans for Grant Proposals or Personal Use

More than half (63.33 percent) of all libraries in the sample offer advice to faculty on how to develop data management plans for grant proposals and/or personal use. This practice is more common among participants in the United States (72.22 percent) than it is among those outside the U.S. (50 percent). Furthermore, the likelihood of a library extending such advice to its faculty increases steadily as full-time equivalent enrollment increases: while just 40 percent of those libraries with less than 15,000 students maintain this practice, this figure jumps to 66.67 percent for the next enrollment range (15,000 to 29,999 students) and then increases once more to 81.82 percent for the top range (30,000 or more). RU/VH and top 150 ranked[3] institutions do this nearly twice as often (81.25 percent) as all other libraries in the sample (42.86 percent).

Training Faculty in Data Management

Just about half (46.67 percent) of all survey participants offer one-on-one tutorials to train faculty in data management. This proves to be the most popular form available to participants. Also utilized, but less popular, are workshops and seminars (used by 36.67 percent of participants), videos or web-based tutorials (23.33 percent), and formal classes (16.67 percent).

Participants in the United States particularly favor the one-on-one tutorials, as 61.11 percent of them use this method to train compared to just 25 percent of libraries in all other countries. These are also more common among larger institutions, with 63.64 percent of those with 30,000 or more students offering one-on-one tutorials compared to just 30 percent of those with less than 15,000 students. Ranking also plays a part, with 62.5 percent of participants in the highest ranking (RU/VH Carnegie Class or equivalent) offer them while just 14.29 percent of all participants listed in the "other" category use them as well.

Formal classes are used by 25 percent of all participants outside the United States, while only 11.11 percent of those in the U.S. use them. This trend is reversed for workshops and seminars, however: 44.44 percent of institutions in the United States use these to train faculty in data management, compared to 25 percent of those outside the U.S. Whereas half of all RU/VH (or top 150 ranked) institutions in the sample offer such workshops or seminars, this is true of only 14.29 percent of all RU/H (or top 400 ranked) participants. For videos and web-based tutorials, usage is more common among the largest universities (with 30,000 or more students) than it is among the smallest ones (less than 15,000 students): 36.36 percent for the former, 10 percent for the latter.

---

[3] See CHARACTERISTICS OF THE SAMPLE section for an explanation of the Carnegie classifications used in this report

RESOURCES FOR DATA CURATION

Library Spending and Grants

We asked survey participants about the library's financial role in supporting data curation at their universities or colleges. Survey participants estimate that a mean of 27.55 percent of the college/university overall spending on data curation is contributed by the library. The range is wide here, however, as three participants cited this figured at 90 percent or higher (two of which said it to be 100 percent) and yet 11 participants said this was 5 percent or lower. This results in an overall median of just 5 percent. The split between United States and all other countries is nearly even (a mean of 27.92 percent for the former and 27 percent for the latter), as are the means for all three enrollment categories, which are all between 26.5 percent and 29 percent. While institutions in the RU/VH (or top 150) and RU/H (or top 400) categories posted a mean between 25 and 26 percent, this figure jumps to a mean of 40 percent for those participants falling under the "other" category here.

Only 13.33 percent of all survey participants say the library has ever received an external grant to support activities in data curation. This is more common among the largest universities (those with 30,000 or more students), as 27.27 percent of these institutions have received such grants, compared to just 10 percent of those with less than 15,000 students and 0 percent of those in the 15,000 to 29,999 student range. This figure raises slightly for countries outside the United States (16.67 percent) and likewise dips a tad for those within the U.S. (11.11 percent).

PERSONNEL

Staff for Data Curation

A bit more than half (56.67 percent) of all survey participants have hired or assigned librarians specifically to work on data curation issues, including 63.64 percent of those with 30,000 or more students. Broken out by country, there is only a slight variation between those participants in the United States (55.56 percent) and those outside the U.S. (58.33 percent). Exactly half of all participants with an FTE enrollment of less than 15,000 have made such hires. Broken out by Carnegie Class (or equivalent), this figure stays between 56.25 and 57.25 percent for all three categories of institutions.

51.72 percent of participants say the library has a data curation staff assigned specifically to deal with this issue. Again, this is more common among the largest universities (63.64 percent of those with enrollment of 30,000 or more) than it is for the smallest (40 percent of those with less than 15,000 students). A wider split emerges here than it has previously when the data is broken out by country: while 55.56 percent of those institutions in the United States have such a data curation staff, as compared to 45.45 percent of those institutions outside the U.S.

For those libraries in the sample that do have a data curation staff, a mean number of 1.83 FTE positions each have been assigned to such departments. The median here is 2, and the range is from a minimum of 0.25 to a max of 4. Countries outside the United States have both a higher mean (2.25 to 1.64) and a higher median (2.5 to 1) than those institutions in the U.S., and this mean steadily drops as enrollment increases: from a mean of 2.67 for those in the "less than 15,000" range, down to 2.17 for those in the "15,000 to 29,999" range and all the way to 1.32 for those in the "30,000 or more" range. Broken out by Carnegie Class, those institutions ranked as RU/H (or in the top 400) posted the lowest mean at 0.75, while the participants that fell in the "other" category posted the highest mean here at 2.33.

Line Item Library Budget for Data Curation

Just 6.67 percent of all survey participants say there is a distinct line item in the library budget for data curation. That is just two participants in the entire sample.

Preparedness of MLS Graduates

Only 20.69 percent of survey participants believe that recent MLS graduates hired by the library have been adequately versed in data curation issues. Those institutions in the United States (16.67 percent) believe these graduates are less prepared than do those institutions outside the U.S. (27.27 percent). The smallest institutions (with less than 15,000 students) are the most positive, with 30 percent saying their MLS graduates are well versed here, compared to just 12.5 percent of those in "15,000 to 29,999" enrollment range. Broken out by Carnegie Class, the survey participants in the "other" are head and shoulders above the rest, with 42.86 percent of them believing their MLS graduates are well prepared, while all other participants in this category fall between 13 and 14.5 percent.

Grant Proposals

For the libraries in the sample, a mean number of 5.66 grant proposals have been reviewed or contributed to by the data curation office in the past year. However, this mean is offset by a few unusually large figures (50 and 45), as the overall median is 0. In fact, outside these two participants, no other library in the sample have more than 13 such grant proposals, and 18 of them have not had any in the past year.

DATA STORAGE

Storing Data Sets

The majority of survey participants (60 percent) store their data sets on the library's server. Another 36 percent store them on some other college or university server, and the remaining 4 percent store them via a cloud computing service. Those institutions with enrollment of less than 15,000 are the most likely to store their data sets on another college or university's server, as 50 percent of them do, compared to 33.33 percent of those in the 15,000 to 29,999 student range and 30 percent of those with 30,000 or more students. RU/VH (or top 150 ranked) institutions favor their own library's server: 73.33 percent of them store their data sets this way, while only 42.86 percent of those participants ranked as RU/H or top 400 do the same.

Integrated Data Set Retrieval

43.48 percent of all survey participants use an open source solution when it comes to integrated data set retrieval, while 34.78 percent have developed their own home-grown approach. The remaining 21.74 percent use a commercial product. These commercial products are more common among institutions in the United States (26.67 percent use them) than they are elsewhere, where just 12.5 percent use them. Likewise, 50 percent of all institutions falling under the "other" category when broken out by Carnegie Class approach integrated data set retrieval with a commercial product, as compared to just 14.29 percent of those classified as RU/VH (or a top 150 ranking).

DATA INTEGRITY

Data Preservation Strategies

Only 20 percent of all survey participants say the library has a data preservation strategy through which it has decided to maintain data for a minimum number of years. These strategies are more common among institutions in the United States (28.57 percent) than they are elsewhere (9.09 percent). While no RU/H (or top 400) institutions have such a strategy in place, a third of all participants in the "other" category here do, as do 23.08 percent of those classified as RU/VH (or top 150).

Ease of Procuring and Archiving Notes or Logs from Scientific/Social Science Experiments

42.86 percent of all survey participants say it has been "very difficult" to procure and archive notes or logs from scientific/social science experiments, the largest number in the sample. Next closest are those who say they have been "able to do with modest challenges," at 21.43 percent. While no institutions outside the U.S. say this has been either "quite easy" or "relatively easy" to do, 33.33 percent of those participants in the U.S. say this is the case. This is also the case for 37.5 percent of all RU/VH (or top 150 ranked) institutions, the only such participants in this category to rate this way.

Ease of Procuring and Archiving Output or Results from Medical or Scientific Instruments or Other Monitors

53.85 percent of all survey participants say it has been "very difficult" to procure and archive output or results from medical or scientific instruments or other monitors, including 75 percent of those participants outside the United States, 100 percent of those in the 15,000 to 29,999 enrollment range, and 100 percent of RU/H (or top 400 ranked) institutions. 100 percent of those listed as "other" in the Carnegie Class breakout also found this to be "very difficult." One anomaly here is in the 30,000 or more enrollment range, where all participants say they are at least "able to do with modest challenges," and 50 percent say they can do this either "quite easily" or "relatively easily."

Ease of Procuring and Archiving Video, Photographs, or Other Images

29.41 percent of all survey participants say they it is "very difficult" to procure and archive video, photographs, and other images, while an identical 29.41 percent say it is either "quite easy" or "relatively easy." Yet another 29.41 percent say they are "able to do with modest challenges." The smallest institutions have generally the most difficult time with this, as 57.17 percent of those with less than 15,000 students and 50 percent of those in the 15,000 to 29,999 enrollment range say it is either "relatively difficult" or "very difficult." On the other side of the coin, just 16.67 percent of those institutions with 30,000 or more students cite this to be the case.

Ease of Procuring and Archiving Spreadsheets

When it comes to procuring and archiving spreadsheets, 31.25 percent of survey participants say this is "very difficult," including 40 percent of those participants outside the U.S. and 66.67 percent of those classified as either RU/H (or top 400) or as "other" in the Carnegie Class breakout category. However, 40 percent of those participants with 30,000 or more students say this is "quite easy."

Ease of Procuring and Archiving Databases

37.5 percent of survey participants say procuring and archiving databases is "very difficult." Broken out by FTE enrollment, those participants in the middle range (15,000 to 29,999 students) have the most difficult time with this, as 75 percent of them say it is "very difficult." Compare this to the 40 percent of those in the "30,000 or more" enrollment range that find this to be either "relatively easy" or "quite easy." Whereas 60 percent of all participants outside the U.S. find this to be either "relatively difficult" or "very difficult," this is the case for 45.45 percent of those participants in the United States.

Ease of Procuring and Archiving Software Code

Nearly half (46.67 percent) of all survey participants find procuring and archiving software code to be "very difficult," including 75 percent of participants outside the U.S. and 75 percent of those in the 15,000 to 29,999 enrollment range. Only 6.67 percent of all participants find this to be "quite easy," all of which are RU/VH (or top 150) institutions with 30,000 or more students.

Ease of Developing Metadata for Notes or Logs from Scientific/Social Science Experiments

35.71 percent of survey participants find it "very difficult" to develop metadata for notes or logs from scientific/social science experiments. There is a bit of a discrepancy when the data is broken out by country, as 37.5 percent of participants in the United States find this either "quite easy" or "relatively easy," compared to just 16.67 percent of those outside the United States. A bit more drastic is the discrepancy when the data is broken out by Carnegie Class, as 50 percent of all those ranked RU/VH (or top 150) find it "quite easy" or "relatively easy," while no other participants rated it this way.

Ease of Developing Metadata for Output or Results from Medical or Scientific Instruments or Other Monitors

Again, 35.71 percent of all survey participants find it "very difficult" to develop metadata for output or results from medical or scientific instruments or other monitors, including 60 percent of those participants outside the U.S. and 66.67 percent of those in the middle enrollment range (15,000 to 29,999 students). On the other end of the spectrum, 60 percent of those institutions with 30,000 or more students say it is either "quite easy" or "relatively easy" to develop such metadata, as do 62.5 percent of those institutions ranked RU/VH (or top 150). No other participants in the Carnegie Class breakout answered the question this way.

Ease of Developing Metadata for Video, Photographs, or Other Images

Half of all survey participants say it is either "quite easy" or "relatively easy" to develop metadata for video, photographs, or other images. Broken out by FTE enrollment, the largest institutions handle this with the most ease, with 66.67 percent saying it is "quite easy" to do so—whereas no other participants rated it this way. While 66.67 percent of all participants categorized as "other" in the Carnegie Class breakout rated this development as "very difficult," 75 percent of those listed as RU/H (or top 400) said it was either "quite easy" or "relatively easy."

Ease of Developing Metadata for Spreadsheets and Databases

Just about half (47.05 percent) of all survey participants say it is either "quite easy" or "relatively easy" to develop metadata for spreadsheets, while 41.17 percent rate developing metadata for databases the same way. When broken out by Carnegie Class, 66.67 of all participants in the "other" category say it is "very difficult" to develop metadata for both spreadsheets and databases, while 60 percent of RU/VH (or top 150) institutions say it is either "quite easy" or "relatively easy" to do the former and 50 percent say the same for the latter.

Ease of Developing Metadata for Software Code

About a third (31.25 percent) of all participants say it is "very difficult" to develop metadata for software code, including 50 percent of those in the 15,000 to 29,999 enrollment range and 66.67 percent of those rated as "other" in the Carnegie Class breakout. A third of all participants with 30,000 or more students find this to be "quite easy." Broken out by country, those participants outside the United States have more difficulty than those participants in the U.S., as 60 percent of the former say it is either "relatively difficult" or "very difficult," compared to just 36.36 percent of the latter group.

1. Relations with Faculty on Data Curation Issues

Table 1.1: Does the library offer advice to faculty on how to develop data management plans for grant proposals or personal use?

	Yes	No
Entire sample	63.33%	36.67%

Table 1.2: Does the library offer advice to faculty on how to develop data management plans for grant proposals or personal use? Broken out by country.

Country	Yes	No
United States	72.22%	27.78%
Other	50.00%	50.00%

Table 1.3: Does the library offer advice to faculty on how to develop data management plans for grant proposals or personal use? Broken out by full-time equivalent enrollment.

Enrollment	Yes	No
Less than 15,000	40.00%	60.00%
15,000 to 29,999	66.67%	33.33%
30,000 or more	81.82%	18.18%

Table 1.4: Does the library offer advice to faculty on how to develop data management plans for grant proposals or personal use? Broken out by Carnegie Class (or equivalent).

Carnegie Class (or Equivalent)	Yes	No
RU/VH or top 150 ranking	81.25%	18.75%
RU/H or top 400 ranking	42.86%	57.14%
Other	42.86%	57.14%

Table 1.5: Does the library offer any one-on-one tutorials to train faculty in data management?

	Yes	No
Entire sample	46.67%	53.33%

Table 1.6: Does the library offer any one-on-one tutorials to train faculty in data management? Broken out by country.

Country	Yes	No
United States	61.11%	38.89%
Other	25.00%	75.00%

Table 1.7: Does the library offer any one-on-one tutorials to train faculty in data management? Broken out by full-time equivalent enrollment.

Enrollment	Yes	No
Less than 15,000	30.00%	70.00%
15,000 to 29,999	44.44%	55.56%
30,000 or more	63.64%	36.36%

Table 1.8: Does the library offer any one-on-one tutorials to train faculty in data management? Broken out by Carnegie Class (or equivalent).

Carnegie Class (or Equivalent)	Yes	No
RU/VH or top 150 ranking	62.50%	37.50%
RU/H or top 400 ranking	42.86%	57.14%
Other	14.29%	85.71%

Table 1.9: Does the library offer any formal classes to train faculty in data management?

	Yes	No
Entire sample	16.67%	83.33%

Table 1.10: Does the library offer any formal classes to train faculty in data management? Broken out by country.

Country	Yes	No
United States	11.11%	88.89%
Other	25.00%	75.00%

Table 1.11: Does the library offer any formal classes to train faculty in data management? Broken out by full-time equivalent enrollment.

Enrollment	Yes	No
Less than 15,000	20.00%	80.00%
15,000 to 29,999	0.00%	100.00%
30,000 or more	27.27%	72.73%

Table 1.12: Does the library offer any formal classes to train faculty in data management? Broken out by Carnegie Class (or equivalent).

Carnegie Class (or Equivalent)	Yes	No
RU/VH or top 150 ranking	25.00%	75.00%
RU/H or top 400 ranking	0.00%	100.00%
Other	14.29%	85.71%

Table 1.13: Does the library offer any workshops or seminars to train faculty in data management?

	Yes	No
Entire sample	36.67%	63.33%

Table 1.14: Does the library offer any workshops or seminars to train faculty in data management? Broken out by country.

Country	Yes	No
United States	44.44%	55.56%
Other	25.00%	75.00%

Table 1.15: Does the library offer any workshops or seminars to train faculty in data management? Broken out by full-time equivalent enrollment.

Enrollment	Yes	No
Less than 15,000	30.00%	70.00%
15,000 to 29,999	33.33%	66.67%
30,000 or more	45.45%	54.55%

Table 1.16: Does the library offer any workshops or seminars to train faculty in data management? Broken out by Carnegie Class (or equivalent).

Carnegie Class (or Equivalent)	Yes	No
RU/VH or top 150 ranking	50.00%	50.00%
RU/H or top 400 ranking	14.29%	85.71%
Other	28.57%	71.43%

Table 1.17: Does the library offer any videos or web-based tutorials to train faculty in data management?

	Yes	No
Entire sample	23.33%	76.67%

Table 1.18: Does the library offer any videos or web-based tutorials to train faculty in data management? Broken out by country.

Country	Yes	No
United States	27.78%	72.22%
Other	16.67%	83.33%

Table 1.19: Does the library offer any videos or web-based tutorials to train faculty in data management? Broken out by full-time equivalent enrollment.

Enrollment	Yes	No
Less than 15,000	10.00%	90.00%
15,000 to 29,999	22.22%	77.78%
30,000 or more	36.36%	63.64%

Table 1.20: Does the library offer any videos or web-based tutorials to train faculty in data management? Broken out by Carnegie Class (or equivalent).

Carnegie Class (or Equivalent)	Yes	No
RU/VH or top 150 ranking	37.50%	62.50%
RU/H or top 400 ranking	14.29%	85.71%
Other	0.00%	100.00%

International Survey of Academic Library Data Curation Practices

Describe your institution's data curation information literacy efforts and support efforts.

1. Nothing.

2. We are providing a workshop over the summer directed at summer research students, but open to faculty. In addition we are providing one-on-one consultation and a libguide with more information.

3. Workshops, web page for graduate students.

4. Outreach through Office of Research, Research Computing and individual departments or faculty. Periodic information sessions on DMPTool.

5. We are developing course, providing workshops for library faculty, providing one-shots, coordinating with IL efforts.

6. Early stages in policy development and analysis of training needs.

7. We are still in a very early stage but we try to answer questions about where and how to make research data available.

8. Extensive.

9. We're in the developmental stages of developing our capabilities.

10. We are hoping to develop services in this area.

11. Data curation is discussed a lot at the library, among researchers and at some levels of university management. There is a general agreement that this is an important issue, but no clear agreement on what should actually be done about it. The library is an important part of these discussions and offer advice based on the skills and knowledge we have. But we do not yet offer any courses or workshops on this issue.

12. We are on the point of offering one or more of the above. We've run workshops with our Library Liaison staff and are now developing a Data Literacy toolkit... watch this space!

13. In consideration at present.

14. Responsibility of the Data Librarian of the LSE with workshops and one and one tutorial to research active staff and research support staff. Early career researchers and PhD level researchers are also targeted for particular support.

15. They provide a special information literacy class for a special subject

16. We are currently developing a series of data management workshops for graduate students and research staff. These will include some aspects of data literacy, but primarily focus on responsible data management practices to facilitate preservation and curation. We also have a data repository for which we are developing policies and procedures to enable data citation, sharing, re-use, and preservation.

17. We are currently assessing the need to develop such a program based upon faculty and curriculum needs and existing resources across campus.

18. We are in the process of defining needs & services and are planning to offer them.

19. Offer individualized consulting on data management plans. Web-based resource center

on data management.

20. VCU Libraries are hiring a Director of Research Data Management.

21. My institution is just starting to develop support services for this.

22. None.

23. We are in the beginning stages and have set up LibGuides, offer one on one tutorials. We are planning for formal classes, workshops.

24. We are just beginning. As part of the University of California system, we can lean on consortial efforts such as UC3.

25. Currently, we have a Data Management website and have linked in with the DMPTool. The library is the first point of contact and depending on the questions, refer to other units on campus. The Library has sponsored several programs around data management, open data, and open science to campus for the past 3 years.

26. We have given talks and demonstrations on data curation tools and tactics.

27. Campus workshops, templates, one-on-one consultation.

28. SLU has spoken at local (university and community) forums on digital preservation and data curation. We are in the process of investigating formal data curation training as an offering.

29. We offer one-on-one consultation to faculty, graduate students and post-docs; a 60-minute workshop in data management; and point-of-service information on our web site. In the fall, we will be offering a credit-bearing graduate-level course in research data management (a 10-week class, 2 credits).

30. In-person workshops (3 varieties), an online course, and recorded sessions. See a list at our website: https://www.lib.umn.edu/datamanagement/workshops

2. Resources for Data Curation

Table 2.1: What percentage of the college/university overall spending on data curation would you say is contributed by the library?

	Mean	Median	Minimum	Maximum
Entire sample	27.55%	5.00%	0.00%	100.00%

Table 2.2: What percentage of the college/university overall spending on data curation would you say is contributed by the library? Broken out by country.

Country	Mean	Median	Minimum	Maximum
United States	27.92%	0.00%	0.00%	100.00%
Other	27.00%	12.50%	0.00%	100.00%

Table 2.3: What percentage of the college/university overall spending on data curation would you say is contributed by the library? Broken out by full-time equivalent enrollment.

Enrollment	Mean	Median	Minimum	Maximum
Less than 15,000	26.67%	10.00%	0.00%	100.00%
15,000 to 29,999	28.57%	5.00%	0.00%	100.00%
30,000 or more	27.29%	5.00%	0.00%	100.00%

Table 2.4: What percentage of the college/university overall spending on data curation would you say is contributed by the library? Broken out by Carnegie Class (or equivalent).

Carnegie Class (or Equivalent)	Mean	Median	Minimum	Maximum
RU/VH or top 150 ranking	25.09%	5.00%	0.00%	100.00%
RU/H or top 400 ranking	25.83%	2.50%	0.00%	100.00%
Other	40.00%	20.00%	0.00%	100.00%

Table 2.5: Has the library ever received an external grant to support activities in data curation?

	Yes	No
Entire sample	13.33%	86.67%

Table 2.6: Has the library ever received an external grant to support activities in data curation? Broken out by country.

Country	Yes	No
United States	11.11%	88.89%
Other	16.67%	83.33%

Table 2.7: Has the library ever received an external grant to support activities in data curation? Broken out by full-time equivalent enrollment.

Enrollment	Yes	No
Less than 15,000	10.00%	90.00%
15,000 to 29,999	0.00%	100.00%
30,000 or more	27.27%	72.73%

Table 2.8: Has the library ever received an external grant to support activities in data curation? Broken out by Carnegie Class (or equivalent).

Carnegie Class (or Equivalent)	Yes	No
RU/VH or top 150 ranking	18.75%	81.25%
RU/H or top 400 ranking	0.00%	100.00%
Other	14.29%	85.71%

Describe your library's relations with other players in data curation, such as the college/university office of grants management, or the academic departments that use the data curation services. Do they understand the library's efforts? Are there turf battles? What is the overall level of cooperation?

1. No role.

2. We have collaborated with the Coordinator of Research Programs in the Office of Academic Affairs. She has worked with us to help us develop outreach and programming to campus. The collaboration has been very balanced and mutually beneficial.

3. Yes, library is understood as the place for data curation. Very cooperative. Office of Sponsored Programs (grants management) refers researchers to the library. Library has done collaborative work with Vice President for Graduate Studies.

4. See answer to earlier question. Good relationship between Office of Research Computing. OK cooperation with Office of Research. So far we've worked with low hanging fruit for academic departments, so really no turf battles.

5. We consult and collaborate with the office of the VP of research. Grants are reported to the library research department. We provide workshops for academic departments.

6. Partnership with Research Office in development of RDM solution and guidance.

7. Generally very good - we work closely with IT and our eResearch Centre.

8. We haven't got that far yet.

9. Good relations with the office of grants management and with the university archive. We are discussing our different responsibilities as regards to data curation. We also have informal discussions with data curation projects going on at the university, particularly as regards to geodata.

10. Working on this right now - growing synergies, positive signs, but takes time - big changes for everyone.

11. I am new in post and RDM services are in development. However inter departmental collaboration is good here and the existing liaison network will provide a firm foundation. Advocacy for the role of the library is needed and I do not anticipate any undue rivalry.

12. We partner with the Office of the Vice Chancellor for Research with regards to funding agency requirements. Regarding educational efforts, we are building partnerships with a variety of campus units, including the Indiana CTSI. We are not currently competing with other units to provide "curation," we are not yet piloting curation services ourselves.

13. We are working with the Office of Sponsored Programs and the National Supercomputing Center to identify existing resources and needs. This phase has been very cordial and collegial.

14. We are just beginning conversations.

15. The Office of the Vice President for Research directs researchers/PIs to the library's data curation services.

16. Cooperating with Office of Research re new position and DMPTool.

17. Since the Library has only just started its efforts, there is not yet great awareness.

18. Conversations are ongoing at the level of the Deans and the UL and Academic Computing.

19. We are just beginning to set up relationships and data curation services. There are no turf battles.

20. Office of Research compliance links to a webpage, but that's it. We are working on a closer collaboration, and think there will be a willingness to do so.

21. We are working closely with the Office of the VP for Research and have met with staff from Sponsored Projects. We worked with Sponsored Project to add text about data management services provided by the library to all new NSF and NIH grant awardees. We also receive messages of new NSF and NIH grant awardees. We have had difficulties getting the word out about data management services to campus, although one of the librarians is chair of the Campus Data Management Committee and the Campus Research Data Governance Committee. We plan on working on this during the summer/fall. We will be providing data management services workshops to faculty and graduate students in the fall.

22. Tepid.

23. Just now starting the conversation with Office of Research, individual faculty, and the Information Science and Technology Center (ISTeC).

24. There has been very little interaction whatsoever.

25. Data curation services are new to our campus and Library. We are working hard to build relationships across campus units. We already work very closely with Information Services, and are growing relationships with the Research Office (which houses the pre- and post-award grant administration services) and the Graduate School. They mostly understand our efforts, and agree that the Library is a natural fit for taking the lead on data management/curation. We have trouble getting the word out to the colleges and departments; we are a very decentralized campus (physically and culturally). Some units have their own IT staff, and don't understand the necessity or scope of the services that we offer (and plan to expand upon). Overall, we have a branding and marketing issue.

26. Poor. We do not cooperate with units on campus. In fact, one unit is hiring a DM specialist of their own.

Since many grants now require a data curation strategy, and many departments of a college may be involved in this effort, the cost of this effort should be shared among these departmental players. Is this the case at your institution? If so, how do the contributions and roles break down? Has the library been given extra funds to carry out its data curation role?

1. No to both.

2. At this point there have been no extra funds, we are able to do our current work with the resources and staff we already have. This may change in the future since we are only in the beginning stages of offering services.

3. Cost is still being considered Currently, its part of institutional infrastructure. No extra funds for curation.

4. This has not been worked out yet.

5. Funds provided for key staff: Policy and Compliance Manager. Research Data Support Officer based in the Library.

6. Yes we do all share the work, couldn't really split the costs, the Library pays for it out of ongoing funds - nothing extra

7. We haven't got that far yet.

8. No extra funding. In fact, as much as we see the need for the library to work with curation of research data, we also hesitate to take such a responsibility without a clear mandate from the university, which either extra funding or a clear priority when compared to other library responsibilities (i.e. work more on data curation, less on collection development).

9. These requirements have not yet impacted in NZ, but we anticipate this will be the case in the near future.

10. Areas still to be discussed, however I think the assumption id for cross departmental collaboration as the role of the library is generally accepted. In practice costs will be shared where necessary but there is no pro rata breakdown of this.

11. We have not yet received additional funds for this role. Currently, we are building a case to demonstrate the value of data management, preservation, and curation activities.

12. While one on one consultations between liaison librarians and other members of the UNLV faculty have taken place, and some faculty have expressed interest in depositing datasets into the institutional repository, no larger role has been identified for the University Libraries, and no funding has been offered or requested.

13. Researchers are not obligated to use the library's data repository, or our consultative services. The library has not been allocated additional funds for our data management/curation/preservation role.

14. Nothing yet.

15. No.

16. No.

17. Nothing has been shared yet among department players. The library has not been given funds.

18. No, we have not been given extra money. We are considering using some one time money to buy a certain amount of space at our consortial repository for future use.

19. No.

20. No extra funding.

21. Here, the individuals fill out grant forms, some with the Libraries help, and for the most part store their own data. The Libraries has not received any additional funding for data curation.

22. The library has not been given extra funds for data curation. I believe that most grant related data curation would be handed through the office of research and development.

23. We agree that everyone should be [financially] contributing to the effort. As yet, the library has received no additional funds, with the exception of support to hire one new faculty member (a Data Management Specialist, me). As we continue to build capacity in data archiving and sharing via our institutional repository, we will need to pursue new models for sustainability (e.g. fee-for-service or extra funds from the university administration).

24. No. We offer support in kind.

Which academic fields would you say take most advantage of the data curation services offered by the library?

1. None.

2. Mostly some of the sciences--chemistry and biology--but we have had some interest from faculty in the humanities.

3. Biology, Environmental Sciences, Education.

4. Public Policy, Computational Social Sciences, Computer Science, Engineering, Conservation Studies. Still lack of awareness on campus...

5. Agriculture and engineering.

6. Hard science - biomed, physics etc.

7. We haven't got that far yet.

8. Today: Fields that use geodata. We see a big need from the social sciences that no one supports or coordinates today.

9. Don't yet know, but most likely to be the 'softer' sciences and humanities.

10. LSE is concerned with Social Science research and RDM services are promoted to all departments.

11. The social sciences and life sciences, thus far.

12. College of Engineering and School of Community Health Sciences.

13. Sciences: engineering, agriculture, environmental sciences.

14. Biosciences.

15. Not yet applicable. Except, we do sometimes get research data submitted with a thesis and so it is packaged into a PDF envelope and loaded into DSpace. There is not extra metadata to identify the data files so bundled into the dissertation. This has happened with a Chemistry PHD dissertation. Also, we do get multimedia files from the Fine Arts doctoral students.

16. Science and medicine.

17. Evolutionary and Ecology Biology. Environmental Studies.

18. We're not sure who is using the Data Management website. Meetings have been held with faculty in optics, astronomy, engineering, pharmacy, and psychology.

19. STEM

20. Engineering, Life Sciences

21. At this point, there are no clear leaders. Students from all colleges and departments attend our workshops. One-on-one services are rarely used by faculty (probably because they aren't aware of them).

22. Sci/Eng. Mostly Chemistry.

3. Personnel

Table 3.1: Have you hired or assigned librarians specifically to work on data curation issues?

	Yes	No
Entire sample	56.67%	43.33%

Table 3.2: Have you hired or assigned librarians specifically to work on data curation issues? Broken out by country.

Country	Yes	No
United States	55.56%	44.44%
Other	58.33%	41.67%

Table 3.3: Have you hired or assigned librarians specifically to work on data curation issues? Broken out by full-time equivalent enrollment.

Enrollment	Yes	No
Less than 15,000	50.00%	50.00%
15,000 to 29,999	55.56%	44.44%
30,000 or more	63.64%	36.36%

Table 3.4: Have you hired or assigned librarians specifically to work on data curation issues? Broken out by Carnegie Class (or equivalent).

Carnegie Class (or Equivalent)	Yes	No
RU/VH or top 150 ranking	56.25%	43.75%
RU/H or top 400 ranking	57.14%	42.86%
Other	57.14%	42.86%

Table 3.5: Does your library have a data curation staff assigned specifically to deal with this issue?

	Yes	No
Entire sample	51.72%	48.28%

Table 3.6: Does your library have a data curation staff assigned specifically to deal with this issue? Broken out by country.

Country	Yes	No
United States	55.56%	44.44%
Other	45.45%	54.55%

Table 3.7: Does your library have a data curation staff assigned specifically to deal with this issue? Broken out by full-time equivalent enrollment.

Enrollment	Yes	No
Less than 15,000	40.00%	60.00%
15,000 to 29,999	50.00%	50.00%
30,000 or more	63.64%	36.36%

Table 3.8: Does your library have a data curation staff assigned specifically to deal with this issue? Broken out by Carnegie Class (or equivalent).

Carnegie Class (or Equivalent)	Yes	No
RU/VH or top 150 ranking	56.25%	43.75%
RU/H or top 400 ranking	33.33%	66.67%
Other	57.14%	42.86%

Table 3.9: If the library has a data curation staff, how many FTE positions have been assigned to this staff or department?

	Mean	Median	Minimum	Maximum
Entire sample	1.83	2.00	0.25	4.00

Table 3.10: If the library has a data curation staff, how many FTE positions have been assigned to this staff or department? Broken out by country.

Country	Mean	Median	Minimum	Maximum
United States	1.64	1.00	0.25	4.00
Other	2.25	2.50	1.00	3.00

Table 3.11: If the library has a data curation staff, how many FTE positions have been assigned to this staff or department? Broken out by full-time equivalent enrollment.

Enrollment	Mean	Median	Minimum	Maximum
Less than 15,000	2.67	3.00	1.00	4.00
15,000 to 29,999	2.17	2.00	1.00	3.50
30,000 or more	1.32	1.00	0.25	3.00

Table 3.12: If the library has a data curation staff, how many FTE positions have been assigned to this staff or department? Broken out by Carnegie Class (or equivalent).

Carnegie Class (or Equivalent)	Mean	Median	Minimum	Maximum
RU/VH or top 150 ranking	1.91	2.00	0.25	3.50
RU/H or top 400 ranking	0.75	0.75	0.50	1.00
Other	2.33	2.00	1.00	4.00

Table 3.13: Is there a distinct line item in your library budget for data curation?

	Yes	No
Entire sample	6.67%	93.33%

Table 3.14: Is there a distinct line item in your library budget for data curation? Broken out by country.

Country	Yes	No
United States	5.56%	94.44%
Other	8.33%	91.67%

Table 3.15: Is there a distinct line item in your library budget for data curation? Broken out by full-time equivalent enrollment.

Enrollment	Yes	No
Less than 15,000	10.00%	90.00%
15,000 to 29,999	0.00%	100.00%
30,000 or more	9.09%	90.91%

Table 3.16: Is there a distinct line item in your library budget for data curation? Broken out by Carnegie Class (or equivalent).

Carnegie Class (or Equivalent)	Yes	No
RU/VH or top 150 ranking	12.50%	87.50%
RU/H or top 400 ranking	0.00%	100.00%
Other	0.00%	100.00%

Table 3.17: Do you believe that recent MLS graduates hired by the library have been adequately versed in data curation issues?

	Yes	No
Entire sample	20.69%	79.31%

Table 3.18: Do you believe that recent MLS graduates hired by the library have been adequately versed in data curation issues? Broken out by country.

Country	Yes	No
United States	16.67%	83.33%
Other	27.27%	72.73%

Table 3.19: Do you believe that recent MLS graduates hired by the library have been adequately versed in data curation issues? Broken out by full-time equivalent enrollment.

Enrollment	Yes	No
Less than 15,000	30.00%	70.00%
15,000 to 29,999	12.50%	87.50%
30,000 or more	18.18%	81.82%

Table 3.20: Do you believe that recent MLS graduates hired by the library have been adequately versed in data curation issues? Broken out by Carnegie Class (or equivalent).

Carnegie Class (or Equivalent)	Yes	No
RU/VH or top 150 ranking	13.33%	86.67%
RU/H or top 400 ranking	14.29%	85.71%
Other	42.86%	57.14%

Table 3.21: What is the total number of grant proposals that have been reviewed or contributed to by your data curation office or service in the past year?

	Mean	Median	Minimum	Maximum
Entire sample	5.66	0.00	0.00	50.00

Table 3.22: What is the total number of grant proposals that have been reviewed or contributed to by your data curation office or service in the past year? Broken out by country.

Country	Mean	Median	Minimum	Maximum
United States	8.94	1.00	0.00	50.00
Other	1.00	0.00	0.00	12.00

Table 3.23: What is the total number of grant proposals that have been reviewed or contributed to by your data curation office or service in the past year? Broken out by full-time equivalent enrollment.

Enrollment	Mean	Median	Minimum	Maximum
Less than 15,000	1.00	0.00	0.00	10.00
15,000 to 29,999	5.78	0.00	0.00	50.00
30,000 or more	10.20	7.50	0.00	45.00

Table 3.24: What is the total number of grant proposals that have been reviewed or contributed to by your data curation office or service in the past year? Broken out by Carnegie Class (or equivalent).

Carnegie Class (or Equivalent)	Mean	Median	Minimum	Maximum
RU/VH or top 150 ranking	8.93	1.00	0.00	50.00
RU/H or top 400 ranking	4.29	0.00	0.00	13.00
Other	0.00	0.00	0.00	0.00

4. Data Storage

Table 4.1: How are your data sets largely stored?

	Cloud computing service	Library's server	Some other college/university server
Entire sample	4.00%	60.00%	36.00%

Table 4.2: How are your data sets largely stored? Broken out by country.

Country	Cloud computing service	Library's server	Some other college/university server
United States	6.25%	62.50%	31.25%
Other	0.00%	55.56%	44.44%

Table 4.3: How are your data sets largely stored? Broken out by full-time equivalent enrollment.

Enrollment	Cloud computing service	Library's server	Some other college/university server
Less than 15,000	0.00%	50.00%	50.00%
15,000 to 29,999	11.11%	55.56%	33.33%
30,000 or more	0.00%	70.00%	30.00%

Table 4.4: How are your data sets largely stored? Broken out by Carnegie Class (or equivalent).

Carnegie Class (or Equivalent)	Cloud computing service	Library's server	Some other college/university server
RU/VH or top 150 ranking	0.00%	73.33%	26.67%
RU/H or top 400 ranking	14.29%	42.86%	42.86%
Other	0.00%	33.33%	66.67%

Table 4.5: How do you approach integrated data set retrieval?

	We use an open source solution	We use a commercial product	We have developed our own home-grown approach
Entire sample	43.48%	21.74%	34.78%

Table 4.6: How do you approach integrated data set retrieval? Broken out by country.

Country	We use an open source solution	We use a commercial product	We have developed our own home-grown approach
United States	46.67%	26.67%	26.67%
Other	37.50%	12.50%	50.00%

Table 4.7: How do you approach integrated data set retrieval? Broken out by full-time equivalent enrollment.

Enrollment	We use an open source solution	We use a commercial product	We have developed our own home-grown approach
Less than 15,000	33.33%	33.33%	33.33%
15,000 to 29,999	42.86%	14.29%	42.86%
30,000 or more	50.00%	20.00%	30.00%

Table 4.8: How do you approach integrated data set retrieval? Broken out by Carnegie Class (or equivalent).

Carnegie Class (or Equivalent)	We use an open source solution	We use a commercial product	We have developed our own home-grown approach
RU/VH or top 150 ranking	50.00%	14.29%	35.71%
RU/H or top 400 ranking	42.86%	28.57%	28.57%
Other	0.00%	50.00%	50.00%

5. Data Integrity

At your institution, have you had any data curation disasters in which critical data was lost, destroyed, impermissibly accessed, or otherwise rendered far less useful than it might have been with more adequate curation measures? Keeping in mind that responses are not connected to institutions or respondents, can you describe some of these instances?

1. No disasters.

2. Not in the library, but faculty have told us of problems they have had (which is why there are interested in getting our help!).

3. Library, no. Researchers have lost data, or data not usable because of older media.

4. Not that I'm aware of.

5. N/A.

6. Fire in one of the University buildings last year.

7. The usual - poor back ups, no back ups, etc.

8. Not known to us but probable.

9. Your questions up to this point are very Yes/No - nothing is quite that simple and most of my responses should really be a combination of your options e.g. previous question - we're currently working on an open source solution, incorporating an in-house build

10. N/A.

11. Main examples gathered so far are isolated examples of sharing amongst academic data that was licensed for single use.

12. Not aware of any

13. No.

14. Not to my knowledge.

15. Yes, I know of people who lost data on DVDs but not on a backed up server.

16. No.

17. We have some scientific data sets sent to Archives when a Prof retired. The format is on tape and is currently not recoverable.

18. No.

19. N/A.

20. No.

21. No.

Table 5.1: Does the library have a data preservation strategy through which it has decided to maintain data for a minimum number of years?

	Yes	No
Entire sample	20.00%	80.00%

Table 5.2: Does the library have a data preservation strategy through which it has decided to maintain data for a minimum number of years? Broken out by country.

Country	Yes	No
United States	28.57%	71.43%
Other	9.09%	90.91%

Table 5.3: Does the library have a data preservation strategy through which it has decided to maintain data for a minimum number of years? Broken out by full-time equivalent enrollment.

Enrollment	Yes	No
Less than 15,000	22.22%	77.78%
15,000 to 29,999	14.29%	85.71%
30,000 or more	22.22%	77.78%

Table 5.4: Does the library have a data preservation strategy through which it has decided to maintain data for a minimum number of years? Broken out by Carnegie Class (or equivalent).

Carnegie Class (or Equivalent)	Yes	No
RU/VH or top 150 ranking	23.08%	76.92%
RU/H or top 400 ranking	0.00%	100.00%
Other	33.33%	66.67%

Table 5.5: How easy has it been to procure and archive notes or logs from scientific/social science experiments?

	Quite easy	Relatively easy	Able to do with modest challenges	Relatively difficult	Very difficult
Entire sample	14.29%	7.14%	21.43%	14.29%	42.86%

Table 5.6: How easy has it been to procure and archive notes or logs from scientific/social science experiments? Broken out by country.

Country	Quite easy	Relatively easy	Able to do with modest challenges	Relatively difficult	Very difficult
United States	22.22%	11.11%	11.11%	22.22%	33.33%
Other	0.00%	0.00%	40.00%	0.00%	60.00%

Table 5.7: How easy has it been to procure and archive notes or logs from scientific/social science experiments? Broken out by full-time equivalent enrollment.

Enrollment	Quite easy	Relatively easy	Able to do with modest challenges	Relatively difficult	Very difficult
Less than 15,000	0.00%	14.29%	28.57%	14.29%	42.86%
15,000 to 29,999	33.33%	0.00%	0.00%	0.00%	66.67%
30,000 or more	25.00%	0.00%	25.00%	25.00%	25.00%

Table 5.8: How easy has it been to procure and archive notes or logs from scientific/social science experiments? Broken out by Carnegie Class (or equivalent).

Carnegie Class (or Equivalent)	Quite easy	Relatively easy	Able to do with modest challenges	Relatively difficult	Very difficult
RU/VH or top 150 ranking	25.00%	12.50%	12.50%	25.00%	25.00%
RU/H or top 400 ranking	0.00%	0.00%	33.33%	0.00%	66.67%
Other	0.00%	0.00%	33.33%	0.00%	66.67%

Table 5.9: How easy has it been to procure and archive output or results from medical or scientific instruments or other monitors?

	Quite easy	Relatively easy	Able to do with modest challenges	Relatively difficult	Very difficult
Entire sample	7.69%	15.38%	15.38%	7.69%	53.85%

Table 5.10: How easy has it been to procure and archive output or results from medical or scientific instruments or other monitors? Broken out by country.

Country	Quite easy	Relatively easy	Able to do with modest challenges	Relatively difficult	Very difficult
United States	11.11%	22.22%	11.11%	11.11%	44.44%
Other	0.00%	0.00%	25.00%	0.00%	75.00%

Table 5.11: How easy has it been to procure and archive output or results from medical or scientific instruments or other monitors? Broken out by full-time equivalent enrollment.

Enrollment	Quite easy	Relatively easy	Able to do with modest challenges	Relatively difficult	Very difficult
Less than 15,000	0.00%	16.67%	0.00%	16.67%	66.67%
15,000 to 29,999	0.00%	0.00%	0.00%	0.00%	100.00%
30,000 or more	25.00%	25.00%	50.00%	0.00%	0.00%

Table 5.12: How easy has it been to procure and archive output or results from medical or scientific instruments or other monitors? Broken out by Carnegie Class (or equivalent).

Carnegie Class (or Equivalent)	Quite easy	Relatively easy	Able to do with modest challenges	Relatively difficult	Very difficult
RU/VH or top 150 ranking	12.50%	25.00%	25.00%	12.50%	25.00%
RU/H or top 400 ranking	0.00%	0.00%	0.00%	0.00%	100.00%
Other	0.00%	0.00%	0.00%	0.00%	100.00%

Table 5.13: How easy has it been to procure and archive video, photographs, or other images?

	Quite easy	Relatively easy	Able to do with modest challenges	Relatively difficult	Very difficult
Entire sample	11.76%	17.65%	29.41%	11.76%	29.41%

Table 5.14: How easy has it been to procure and archive video, photographs, or other images? Broken out by country.

Country	Quite easy	Relatively easy	Able to do with modest challenges	Relatively difficult	Very difficult
United States	9.09%	18.18%	45.45%	9.09%	18.18%
Other	16.67%	16.67%	0.00%	16.67%	50.00%

Table 5.15: How easy has it been to procure and archive video, photographs, or other images? Broken out by full-time equivalent enrollment.

Enrollment	Quite easy	Relatively easy	Able to do with modest challenges	Relatively difficult	Very difficult
Less than 15,000	0.00%	14.29%	28.57%	14.29%	42.86%
15,000 to 29,999	0.00%	25.00%	25.00%	0.00%	50.00%
30,000 or more	33.33%	16.67%	33.33%	16.67%	0.00%

Table 5.16: How easy has it been to procure and archive video, photographs, or other images? Broken out by Carnegie Class (or equivalent).

Carnegie Class (or Equivalent)	Quite easy	Relatively easy	Able to do with modest challenges	Relatively difficult	Very difficult
RU/VH or top 150 ranking	10.00%	30.00%	30.00%	20.00%	10.00%
RU/H or top 400 ranking	25.00%	0.00%	50.00%	0.00%	25.00%
Other	0.00%	0.00%	0.00%	0.00%	100.00%

Table 5.17: How easy has it been to procure and archive spreadsheets?

	Quite easy	Relatively easy	Able to do with modest challenges	Relatively difficult	Very difficult
Entire sample	18.75%	25.00%	12.50%	12.50%	31.25%

Table 5.18: How easy has it been to procure and archive spreadsheets? Broken out by country.

Country	Quite easy	Relatively easy	Able to do with modest challenges	Relatively difficult	Very difficult
United States	18.18%	27.27%	18.18%	9.09%	27.27%
Other	20.00%	20.00%	0.00%	20.00%	40.00%

Table 5.19: How easy has it been to procure and archive spreadsheets? Broken out by full-time equivalent enrollment.

Enrollment	Quite easy	Relatively easy	Able to do with modest challenges	Relatively difficult	Very difficult
Less than 15,000	14.29%	28.57%	0.00%	14.29%	42.86%
15,000 to 29,999	0.00%	50.00%	0.00%	0.00%	50.00%
30,000 or more	40.00%	0.00%	40.00%	20.00%	0.00%

Table 5.20: How easy has it been to procure and archive spreadsheets? Broken out by Carnegie Class (or equivalent).

Carnegie Class (or Equivalent)	Quite easy	Relatively easy	Able to do with modest challenges	Relatively difficult	Very difficult
RU/VH or top 150 ranking	20.00%	40.00%	10.00%	20.00%	10.00%
RU/H or top 400 ranking	0.00%	0.00%	33.33%	0.00%	66.67%
Other	33.33%	0.00%	0.00%	0.00%	66.67%

Table 5.21: How easy has it been to procure and archive databases?

	Quite easy	Relatively easy	Able to do with modest challenges	Relatively difficult	Very difficult
Entire sample	12.50%	12.50%	25.00%	12.50%	37.50%

Table 5.22: How easy has it been to procure and archive databases? Broken out by country.

Country	Quite easy	Relatively easy	Able to do with modest challenges	Relatively difficult	Very difficult
United States	9.09%	9.09%	36.36%	9.09%	36.36%
Other	20.00%	20.00%	0.00%	20.00%	40.00%

Table 5.23: How easy has it been to procure and archive databases? Broken out by full-time equivalent enrollment.

Enrollment	Quite easy	Relatively easy	Able to do with modest challenges	Relatively difficult	Very difficult
Less than 15,000	14.29%	14.29%	14.29%	14.29%	42.86%
15,000 to 29,999	0.00%	0.00%	25.00%	0.00%	75.00%
30,000 or more	20.00%	20.00%	40.00%	20.00%	0.00%

Table 5.24: How easy has it been to procure and archive databases? Broken out by Carnegie Class (or equivalent).

Carnegie Class (or Equivalent)	Quite easy	Relatively easy	Able to do with modest challenges	Relatively difficult	Very difficult
RU/VH or top 150 ranking	10.00%	20.00%	30.00%	20.00%	20.00%
RU/H or top 400 ranking	0.00%	0.00%	33.33%	0.00%	66.67%
Other	33.33%	0.00%	0.00%	0.00%	66.67%

Table 5.25: How easy has it been to procure and archive software code?

	Quite easy	Relatively easy	Able to do with modest challenges	Relatively difficult	Very difficult
Entire sample	6.67%	13.33%	20.00%	13.33%	46.67%

Table 5.26: How easy has it been to procure and archive software code? Broken out by country.

Country	Quite easy	Relatively easy	Able to do with modest challenges	Relatively difficult	Very difficult
United States	9.09%	18.18%	18.18%	18.18%	36.36%
Other	0.00%	0.00%	25.00%	0.00%	75.00%

Table 5.27: How easy has it been to procure and archive software code? Broken out by full-time equivalent enrollment.

Enrollment	Quite easy	Relatively easy	Able to do with modest challenges	Relatively difficult	Very difficult
Less than 15,000	0.00%	0.00%	33.33%	16.67%	50.00%
15,000 to 29,999	0.00%	25.00%	0.00%	0.00%	75.00%
30,000 or more	20.00%	20.00%	20.00%	20.00%	20.00%

Table 5.28: How easy has it been to procure and archive software code? Broken out by Carnegie Class (or equivalent).

Carnegie Class (or Equivalent)	Quite easy	Relatively easy	Able to do with modest challenges	Relatively difficult	Very difficult
RU/VH or top 150 ranking	11.11%	22.22%	11.11%	22.22%	33.33%
RU/H or top 400 ranking	0.00%	0.00%	33.33%	0.00%	66.67%
Other	0.00%	0.00%	33.33%	0.00%	66.67%

Table 5.29: How easy has it been to develop metadata for notes or logs from scientific/social science experiments?

	Quite easy	Relatively easy	Able to do with modest challenges	Relatively difficult	Very difficult
Entire sample	7.14%	21.43%	14.29%	21.43%	35.71%

Table 5.30: How easy has it been to develop metadata for notes or logs from scientific/social science experiments? Broken out by country.

Country	Quite easy	Relatively easy	Able to do with modest challenges	Relatively difficult	Very difficult
United States	12.50%	25.00%	12.50%	12.50%	37.50%
Other	0.00%	16.67%	16.67%	33.33%	33.33%

Table 5.31: How easy has it been to develop metadata for notes or logs from scientific/social science experiments? Broken out by full-time equivalent enrollment.

Enrollment	Quite easy	Relatively easy	Able to do with modest challenges	Relatively difficult	Very difficult
Less than 15,000	0.00%	28.57%	14.29%	28.57%	28.57%
15,000 to 29,999	0.00%	33.33%	0.00%	0.00%	66.67%
30,000 or more	25.00%	0.00%	25.00%	25.00%	25.00%

Table 5.32: How easy has it been to develop metadata for notes or logs from scientific/social science experiments? Broken out by Carnegie Class (or equivalent).

Carnegie Class (or Equivalent)	Quite easy	Relatively easy	Able to do with modest challenges	Relatively difficult	Very difficult
RU/VH or top 150 ranking	12.50%	37.50%	12.50%	12.50%	25.00%
RU/H or top 400 ranking	0.00%	0.00%	33.33%	33.33%	33.33%
Other	0.00%	0.00%	0.00%	33.33%	66.67%

Table 5.33: How easy has it been to develop metadata for output or results from medical or scientific instruments or other monitors?

	Quite easy	Relatively easy	Able to do with modest challenges	Relatively difficult	Very difficult
Entire sample	7.14%	28.57%	14.29%	14.29%	35.71%

Table 5.34: How easy has it been to develop metadata for output or results from medical or scientific instruments or other monitors? Broken out by country.

Country	Quite easy	Relatively easy	Able to do with modest challenges	Relatively difficult	Very difficult
United States	11.11%	33.33%	22.22%	11.11%	22.22%
Other	0.00%	20.00%	0.00%	20.00%	60.00%

Table 5.35: How easy has it been to develop metadata for output or results from medical or scientific instruments or other monitors? Broken out by full-time equivalent enrollment.

Enrollment	Quite easy	Relatively easy	Able to do with modest challenges	Relatively difficult	Very difficult
Less than 15,000	0.00%	16.67%	16.67%	33.33%	33.33%
15,000 to 29,999	0.00%	33.33%	0.00%	0.00%	66.67%
30,000 or more	20.00%	40.00%	20.00%	0.00%	20.00%

Table 5.36: How easy has it been to develop metadata for output or results from medical or scientific instruments or other monitors? Broken out by Carnegie Class (or equivalent).

Carnegie Class (or Equivalent)	Quite easy	Relatively easy	Able to do with modest challenges	Relatively difficult	Very difficult
RU/VH or top 150 ranking	12.50%	50.00%	12.50%	12.50%	12.50%
RU/H or top 400 ranking	0.00%	0.00%	33.33%	0.00%	66.67%
Other	0.00%	0.00%	0.00%	33.33%	66.67%

Table 5.37: How easy has it been to develop metadata for video, photographs, or other images?

	Quite easy	Relatively easy	Able to do with modest challenges	Relatively difficult	Very difficult
Entire sample	25.00%	25.00%	18.75%	6.25%	25.00%

Table 5.38: How easy has it been to develop metadata for video, photographs, or other images? Broken out by country.

Country	Quite easy	Relatively easy	Able to do with modest challenges	Relatively difficult	Very difficult
United States	20.00%	30.00%	20.00%	10.00%	20.00%
Other	33.33%	16.67%	16.67%	0.00%	33.33%

Table 5.39: How easy has it been to develop metadata for video, photographs, or other images? Broken out by full-time equivalent enrollment.

Enrollment	Quite easy	Relatively easy	Able to do with modest challenges	Relatively difficult	Very difficult
Less than 15,000	0.00%	28.57%	28.57%	14.29%	28.57%
15,000 to 29,999	0.00%	33.33%	0.00%	0.00%	66.67%
30,000 or more	66.67%	16.67%	16.67%	0.00%	0.00%

Table 5.40: How easy has it been to develop metadata for video, photographs, or other images? Broken out by Carnegie Class (or equivalent).

Carnegie Class (or Equivalent)	Quite easy	Relatively easy	Able to do with modest challenges	Relatively difficult	Very difficult
RU/VH or top 150 ranking	33.33%	11.11%	33.33%	11.11%	11.11%
RU/H or top 400 ranking	25.00%	50.00%	0.00%	0.00%	25.00%
Other	0.00%	33.33%	0.00%	0.00%	66.67%

International Survey of Academic Library Data Curation Practices

Table 5.41: How easy has it been to develop metadata for spreadsheets?

	Quite easy	Relatively easy	Able to do with modest challenges	Relatively difficult	Very difficult
Entire sample	11.76%	35.29%	11.76%	17.65%	23.53%

Table 5.42: How easy has it been to develop metadata for spreadsheets? Broken out by country.

Country	Quite easy	Relatively easy	Able to do with modest challenges	Relatively difficult	Very difficult
United States	18.18%	36.36%	9.09%	18.18%	18.18%
Other	0.00%	33.33%	16.67%	16.67%	33.33%

Table 5.43: How easy has it been to develop metadata for spreadsheets? Broken out by full-time equivalent enrollment.

Enrollment	Quite easy	Relatively easy	Able to do with modest challenges	Relatively difficult	Very difficult
Less than 15,000	0.00%	42.86%	14.29%	14.29%	28.57%
15,000 to 29,999	0.00%	50.00%	0.00%	0.00%	50.00%
30,000 or more	33.33%	16.67%	16.67%	33.33%	0.00%

Table 5.44: How easy has it been to develop metadata for spreadsheets? Broken out by Carnegie Class (or equivalent).

Carnegie Class (or Equivalent)	Quite easy	Relatively easy	Able to do with modest challenges	Relatively difficult	Very difficult
RU/VH or top 150 ranking	20.00%	40.00%	10.00%	20.00%	10.00%
RU/H or top 400 ranking	0.00%	25.00%	25.00%	25.00%	25.00%
Other	0.00%	33.33%	0.00%	0.00%	66.67%

Table 5.45: How easy has it been to develop metadata for databases?

	Quite easy	Relatively easy	Able to do with modest challenges	Relatively difficult	Very difficult
Entire sample	11.76%	29.41%	17.65%	17.65%	23.53%

Table 5.46: How easy has it been to develop metadata for databases? Broken out by country.

Country	Quite easy	Relatively easy	Able to do with modest challenges	Relatively difficult	Very difficult
United States	18.18%	27.27%	18.18%	18.18%	18.18%
Other	0.00%	33.33%	16.67%	16.67%	33.33%

Table 5.47: How easy has it been to develop metadata for databases? Broken out by full-time equivalent enrollment.

Enrollment	Quite easy	Relatively easy	Able to do with modest challenges	Relatively difficult	Very difficult
Less than 15,000	0.00%	28.57%	28.57%	14.29%	28.57%
15,000 to 29,999	0.00%	50.00%	0.00%	0.00%	50.00%
30,000 or more	33.33%	16.67%	16.67%	33.33%	0.00%

Table 5.48: How easy has it been to develop metadata for databases? Broken out by Carnegie Class (or equivalent).

Carnegie Class (or Equivalent)	Quite easy	Relatively easy	Able to do with modest challenges	Relatively difficult	Very difficult
RU/VH or top 150 ranking	20.00%	30.00%	20.00%	20.00%	10.00%
RU/H or top 400 ranking	0.00%	25.00%	25.00%	25.00%	25.00%
Other	0.00%	33.33%	0.00%	0.00%	66.67%

Table 5.49: How easy has it been to develop metadata for software code?

	Quite easy	Relatively easy	Able to do with modest challenges	Relatively difficult	Very difficult
Entire sample	12.50%	18.75%	25.00%	12.50%	31.25%

Table 5.50: How easy has it been to develop metadata for software code? Broken out by country.

Country	Quite easy	Relatively easy	Able to do with modest challenges	Relatively difficult	Very difficult
United States	18.18%	18.18%	27.27%	9.09%	27.27%
Other	0.00%	20.00%	20.00%	20.00%	40.00%

Table 5.51: How easy has it been to develop metadata for software code? Broken out by full-time equivalent enrollment.

Enrollment	Quite easy	Relatively easy	Able to do with modest challenges	Relatively difficult	Very difficult
Less than 15,000	0.00%	16.67%	33.33%	16.67%	33.33%
15,000 to 29,999	0.00%	50.00%	0.00%	0.00%	50.00%
30,000 or more	33.33%	0.00%	33.33%	16.67%	16.67%

Table 5.52: How easy has it been to develop metadata for software code? Broken out by Carnegie Class (or equivalent).

Carnegie Class (or Equivalent)	Quite easy	Relatively easy	Able to do with modest challenges	Relatively difficult	Very difficult
RU/VH or top 150 ranking	22.22%	22.22%	22.22%	11.11%	22.22%
RU/H or top 400 ranking	0.00%	0.00%	50.00%	25.00%	25.00%
Other	0.00%	33.33%	0.00%	0.00%	66.67%

How have you gone about developing metadata for your data curation efforts?

1. We haven't.

2. Use MODS/DC for out repository (Fedora/Hydra based).

3. Work with metadata specialist in cataloging department.

4. We have a metadata librarian.

5. Planning stage - would be keen to see developments in other HEIs.

6. We haven't got that far yet.

7. We have not yet done this.

8. Developing in house protocols and absorbing external guidelines from national and international archives.

9. Extensive research and effort to extend our MODS metadata for research data.

10. Examined approaches from national and international authoritative sources.

11. Not yet a strategic priority for our library.

12. Have not yet started.

13. Collaboratively.

14. Investigating the literature and recommended best practices.

15. Keeping in mind that we have not archived all of the data types that are listed above (and I wasn't given the option to select 'n/a'), developing metadata for datasets has been achieved on a case-by-case basis in partnership with the data contributor. That has been an enjoyable process, as most researchers have been relieved to finally 'get' what metadata is all about, and how easy it can be to create. The more difficult process has been selecting a metadata schema for datasets that is amenable to the restrictions of our repository platform, which has limited, non-hierarchical metadata capabilities.

16. Working closely with the user to develop readme files to accompany the data.

6. Assessment and Information Resources

How have your library's data curation activities impacted the standing and scholarly results of your institution? Have you made efforts to assess the impact of the data curation activities on institutional success?

1. No impact; no assessment: we just don't do data curation as an organization. Each unit department, division or program does their own.

2. Things are still too recent to tell, but we did have a faculty get her NSF grant funded after helping her with writing her data management plan.

3. Have not assessed impact of data curation efforts.

4. No, too early yet.

5. We are investigating a program.

6. Too early in our development of an RDM plan to answer.

7. We think we have done quite well - our Crystallographers are seen as world leading for instance, with this as a contribution.

8. We haven't got that far yet.

9. Only time will tell.

10. Too early to judge. Mechanisms will be put in place to evaluate this soon.

11. We are investigating creation of data curation services in order to enhance the research infrastructure of the institution. We have not designed assessment of this impact as of yet.

12. This is a relatively new activity, and we have not assessed the impact.

13. Nothing yet, we hope new position will fill this role.

14. Since we have only just started the process, it is too early to tell.

15. Not yet a strategic priority for our library.

16. This is not known. No.

17. In progress.

18. It is too early to assess the impacts of our services.

19. No.

What are some of the data archives or directories that you have found most useful in your data curation pursuits?

1. ICPSR.

2. ICPSR, Dataverse, UK Data Archive, Australian National Data Service, Databib.

3. Databib.

4. For information Edinburgh DataShare.

5. Sherpa-Juliet,

6. Svensk Nationell Dataservice http://snd.gu.se/ Environment Climate Data Sweden http://www.smhi.se/ecds

7. Not currently looking at external data archives.

8. Guidelines from Digital Curation Center, Oxford DMP Online, Edinburgh Data Library (Mantra) and UK Data Archive.

9. ICPSR.

10. Digital Curation Center (DCC) Disciplinary Repositories (Purdue D2C2).

11. ICPSR.

12. Databib, Datacite, data.gov http://oad.simmons.edu/oadwiki/Data_repositories

13. DataBib, Dryad.

14. D2C2.

15. Everything coming out of the UKDA has been excellent. Training modules and materials from the US DataONE project have been helpful. The Lamar Soutter Library, University of Massachusetts Medical School: Scientific Research Data Management course information and resources, syllabus, activities and lecture slides.

16. I have not used it but would imagine databib would be useful.

Which blogs, listservs, websites, magazines, newsletters, conferences, and other information resources have you found most useful in your data curation activities?

1. ACRL, ACRL Digital Curation Interest Group, DataOne, UK Data Archive, Digital Curation Centre, as well as a number of libguides from different libraries.

2. See my site I created: https://sites.google.com/site/dmsocialnetworks/ And Zotero Group: https://www.zotero.org/groups/ufloridatraining/items

3. IASSIST, RDAP.

4. DCC, Oxford, Edinburgh and other HEIs pages.

5. ands-general, ands-partners, RESEARCH-DATAMAN@JISCMAIL.AC UK, eResearch Australasia, IDCC.

6. ANDS, DCC News, Tim Berners-Lee, Library Society of the World, Twitter, Library Loon.

7. DCC, JISC, ANDS - mostly the UK and Australian ones.

8. Jisc mail lists.

9. DataONE materials, DDI website, ICPSR website, ACRL 2013, California DPL.

10. Checklist from MIT Libraries Elements and Framework of DMP from ICPSR DMPTool (UCCC/CDL) D-Lib magazine - special issue on research data, January/February 2011

11. Digital Curation Center website, RCUK

12. I monitor many. Perhaps Co-Data is most interesting.

13. Research Data Curation Bibliography Digital Curation Bibliography: Preservation and Stewardship of Scholarly Works E-science and Academic Libraries Bibliography Digital Curation Resource Guide

14. ACRL-Digital Curation Interest Group, RDAP, STS, Research Data management, ICPSR

15. Journal of Library Administration, Computers in Libraries, Journal of Web Librarianship, College and Research Libraries

16. I love Carly Strasser's blog, DataPub: http://datapub.cdlib.org/ The ACRL Data Curation Interest group listserv is interesting, as well as the RESEARCH-DATAMAN listserv from Jisc.

17. arl-data-sharing; IDCC, RDAP

Which institutions do you most admire for their data curation efforts?

1. We admire any institution that has the budget, personnel and time to do it.

2. Purdue, MIT, University of Oregon, UNC, UVA.

3. Purdue, Cornell, UCSD.

4. Monash, Edinburgh, Southampton.

5. Johns Hopkins, Edinburgh, Griffith Uni, Uni of Melbourne, Oxford.

6. Digital Curation Centre, UC-Berkeley, Oxford, Monash, Edinburgh, Newcastle (Australia).

7. Don't know enough yet to admire any particular institution. We currently admire anyone who actually does anything.

8. Places in Australia, like Griffiths, Melbourne and in the UK, St Andrews, Oxford - it's all very fluid and dynamic. Don't know so much about the USA institutions

9. Australian universities.

10. Edinburgh University, University of Leicester, UK Data Archive.

11. MIT, UC Berkeley, Purdue.

12. Digital Curation Center (DCC).

13. Johns Hopkins, Purdue.

14. University of Toronto and U Alberta (in Canada).

15. Purdue, Johns Hopkins, CDL.

16. Penn State University, Purdue, University of Virginia, University of Wisconsin, Univ. of Minnesota, California Digital Library, University of Illinois, Champaign-Urbana

17. Stanford and UT Austin.

18. Purdue.

19. Purdue University, University of Virginia, Johns Hopkins University, Woods Hole Oceanographic Institute (via their Library), Cornell.

20. I don't think anyone has it figured out yet. I look at EarthCube, DataOne, and other scientific data repository networks. Also, SEAD virtual archive has promise.

Made in the USA
Charleston, SC
14 July 2013